T0077999

FORGIVE ME MY EXCUSES HAVE MERCY ON MY REPERCUSSIONS

(ETHICAL RESPONSIBILITY)

ANTONIO A. BURDETTE

Order this book online at www.trafford.com
or email orders@trafford.com

Most Trafford titles are also available at major online book retailers.

© Copyright 2022 Antonio A. Burdette.
All rights reserved. No part of this publication may be reproduced, stored in a retrieval
system, or transmitted, in any form or by any means, electronic, mechanical, photocopying,
recording, or otherwise, without the written prior permission of the author.

Print information available on the last page.

ISBN: 978-1-6987-1108-9 (sc)
ISBN: 978-1-6987-1107-2 (e)

Because of the dynamic nature of the Internet, any web addresses or links contained in
this book may have changed since publication and may no longer be valid. The views
expressed in this work are solely those of the author and do not necessarily reflect the
views of the publisher, and the publisher hereby disclaims any responsibility for them.

Any people depicted in stock imagery provided by Getty Images are models, and such images are
being used for illustrative purposes only.
Certain stock imagery © Getty Images.

Trafford rev. 03/18/2022

www.trafford.com
North America & international
toll-free: 844-688-6899 (USA & Canada)
fax: 812 355 4082

WHAT I'VE FOUNDED OUT as an author its really difficult to gain a readers undivided attention. I also founded out being truthful to who I am leaves no room to question where I'm going!

This book I will make it a special edition to my collection. No main topic will be the focal point just good insight and valuable conversation to whoever decides to pick up this book and thumb through its contents.

I desire for this book to become a best friend that you might not have giving you worthy insights and advice and the enlightening energy to always think first about your blessings and not the everyday hurdles that try to intervene in our everyday lives.

Later in life I founded out that you can't make yourself happy if you never try to improve someone else's life.

Now that the generational era has introduced itself we find ourselves embracing lyrics in songs that touches out heart and deeply relates to out situations or circumstances making it easier to reset our mood.

"I'm Kojak, and I go by tha' Lord most decorative angel." It's a title which reveals my work ethic and how consistent of a spirit I am.

It takes a lot of study time. It takes separating yourself from unannounced company who just wants to ramble your thoughts with what happen over the weekend and social media most current events.

Knowledge is like carrying multiple grocery bags knowin' you only have (2) hands but you manage to grab them all and when you reach your destination you think it's best to ask for help like anything else trying to gain too much knowledge can become overwhelming. For someone who spent a portion of their growing up in the streets and worked around the clock I find writing principles is a bit liberating. Even though I was faced with a lot of unwelcome circumstances I most certainly could've handled them differently. But by putting the pen to the paper it gave me the drive to ask for your blessing of hearing me out in this manner in a longevity way. It's extremely hard making the necessary transitioning to be Christ-like and being human witnessing unlawful crimes headline the news knowing that you have an opinion and can easily get in your feelings but that can't be the reason to stop loving someone or someone else's a lot of insights that make sense to me might not make the same sense to you or anyone else and that's perfectly fine because we are entitled to an opinion.

Even though we tend to solve our own problems and give ourselves self-inflicting advice someone else's lessons and experiences make for the best changes and with a broad nationwide circle of authors the most accurate advice are in books. Me, personally, I like moving and living in a timeless manner. It eliminates rushing to do anything.

You can take the safest way home all the time sooner or later more traffic will become that route. If you live in a city where it's a little countryish don't be so quick to move to a much bigger city. You will be faced with longer grocery store lines, public assistance lines, hospital waits, lottery playing, high velocity of traffic, high volume crime in whatever apartment complex you choose sometimes it's best to just settle until a later time because everyone is not a fan off population because population is known for bringing bout ignorance. I always find it necessary to mention single mothers. You have strengthened every bone that makes up your spinal cord. I see it in the everyday work place how you just don't acknowledge anymore that you're tired or that the mailbox won't be holding a check when you gather the mail. So with all due respect you can't be considered the weakest link and I admire your womanly determination. I acknowledge you because it seems no one ever sees her struggle to help ease that pressure. Added car services has come along making it easier to get around without hurting your wallet and the services could not have come along at a better time. Because nothing stays the same you must develop other ways to make an income I learnt not to involve to many in projects that I'm working on mainly because no one has my best of interest like me what seems like enough for them isn't always enough for me and without a shadow of a doubt there will always be a conflict of interest meaning two different individuals will become incompatible, and its proven time after time to hurt businesses and have proposals refused.

If you have crushed the can and broken the bottle allow me to excitedly speak on sobriety. As I'm moving forward into my fourth year of being clean and sober the first step you have to do is leave the ones alone you conducted your business with you making a transition they not and they will still be there to offer you. The second step you gotta desire it no one can convince you about a cleaner, healthier life and third seek for good supporters because you will always be exposed to the drinks and the affordable substances and set a short goal of one year and I promise you you'll see how sharp your motor skills become.

Has someone death made you question God or made you feel like you can just live without acknowledging. For me it's a yes because of all the untimely deaths that has taken place just in the city where I reside I question God's method why he allow an 8 year old to become a victim of a drive-by shooting and two days later families grieving over love ones loss in a car collision and house fires. I most certainly was brought up to never question God and I don't won't others to let that be my way of thinking

I want people to reel me back in giving me the assurance that I need knowing that God never stop loving.

Whenever you have the free will to do anything such as consuming alcohol you will most certainly bypass the cut off period to give it a rest and the reason being "The Act of Normalcy" it's a basic act but it can also become an indecisive method to support your triggers. Doing anything in a normal fashion it allows you to build trust in its stages of acceptance. There are times when I feel like blessings are just rewards when all I really want is a God that's gonna manufacture my thinking process totally under His will. For instant water is a blessing, fire is a blessing, bleach is a blessing. But we are repeating the act of blessing the body instead of excepting the sacrifice of the body being blessed. Being blessed is to have unlimited praise and conversation with a spiritual orb which dwells on your inside. But to have God totally manufacture you along with what's dwelling on the inside of you working day in and day out manifesting peace that you may live beyond your life unexpected timeline.

The more unhealthy chemicals that you intentionally invite into your body such as nicotine, and the drug known as hash the word of God warns us and gives us the power to cast out unclean spirits that only wants to take over your body using you for the bone marrow that collect what entices them to live.

Everything that goes in negative that takes years to be broken down if you didn't know everything feeds off of something for instant mold grows where things stay moist but over due time it gets into your airwaves, it find where it can breathe and it gives the lungs hell making it difficult to breathe.

Why do bad things happen to good people it's an unexplained logic that I still can't get a satisfying answer for God who is far more supreme than the human anatomy He set the day in time that he wanted to create an image that He wanted to see move in a functional manner. He made the angels also but made them slightly different to give Him praise at all times by voicing them and that's really the duty of them even though we know of them to rescue us at times if only we would have took the freewill to just bow our heads out of respect instead of looking at one another as if we were a simple make clay, water, and air. The things we know about now but didn't at one point. I've always founded angels to be fascinating maybe because they were made before man but I came to realize that their work ethic is to give Him praise by voicing that He's Holy God

Almighty and Jesus was sent for mankind for man to do the job of rescuing by becoming His earthly angels which He called Apostles but yet He came, He lived, he taught, He healed and He died without one becoming angelic and because they fail to obey for a second time we perish.

I'm reaching the age of maturity where I feel good conversation is more rewarding than having disagreements and arguments. To have good conversation that means you have to surround yourself around good people and if you can't deliver good conversation why is you even in my circle only to prove that you're the negative energy. Throughout my years of living even to the best of my ability I notice how difficult it is for others to love one another even the ones who we trust to marry has shown otherwise the ones who supposed to be there to protect and provide has shown us that what was to be the most simplest way of affection will and has gone wrong to put more emphasis on it, it's almost a slap to the chosen Messiah by saying if you're not here to teach and manifest it, it ain't happening and on the other hand there are us who took baby steps to show and tell love just from the values we were taught but time after time we see the races appearing more violently in the news in the worst way so no one wanna take that chance.

In life there will be times when you have to tolerate the people you are around without actually having a bond or close connection with. Apparently we can't make the world or even our country what it has the capability to become because everyone is so caught up in the mischief that nothing good can come from. I've come to the conclusion whenever you write a book it's really up to the readers to determine if the books content will be taught in classes and brought into the home but whatever you do, do it in truth and with a genuine heart and feel confident that it was written to help heal another. It doesn't matter your nationality you control if you want someone other than yourself to love you it's nothing that can happen in an instant you have to gain people's trust and that's just to be considered… and asking my readers to consider trust in me isn't a gamble it's a step in the right direction. What young developing minds have to realize is that people don't try to persuade or influence them in the presence of adults but the right parental advice can make all the difference in their decision-making.

When a person makes a decision to contemplate suicidal thoughts it clearly the encounters had that much influences to override the child's normalcy and later causes the parent to cry out in question and disbelief.

This is a special edition I'm adding to my collection because I want the reader to read in the tones of what concern feel like I want them to see that my hurt didn't claim victory over my life because I one day was gonna get tired and let my guard down. This is a book of insights and conversation as if I was sitting next to someone on a greyhound or airplane. It's me giving thought out answers to my psychologist without jumping around feeling like I'm just complaining. The more I learn how to release pressure from building up my books will become self-explanatory I'm not an individual who wants followers I rather have you say I contributed to a healthier you. When you coming from where I've been and you know what stayed in your system year round cut your child some slack because the only thing that they know is that their normal. I desire for this book to earn book critics respect that my thoughts, my purpose and my values are not just for one people or one race it's to work a mighty motivational breakthrough in someone's life.

What amazes me more than anything is how I manage to break the stronghold from excepting everything that was being offered to me to wanting to embrace another human being unconditionally. What amazes me even more is I allowed my leadership qualities to be stripped from me right from under my nose failing to acknowledge it. I always wanted someone to ask me this why a book? And not a short film or documentary. I chose a book because what I'm relieving from years of enduring it needs to be said in word format. Just as the earth gives us minerals and resources a book is a resource and a reader has to breakdown and study the minerals (content) to see how it can be used.

Short films are used to relay a message quickly to an individual mainly because the eyes have shown to be less wiser than the tongue. Television has challenge books for years what the eyes absorb it's quickly displayed through one's appearance and behavior. Whereas a book is read its content is being relayed to membranes for a righteous concept of understanding and an author should feel compelled on wording a book to someone's understanding. Moses received God's laws by Him writing on tablets of stone which are considered the earliest of literature. Some will choose to take shortcuts and we know why I'm basic, old fashion, and a graduate and yes I carried a backpack with 8 or more books that certainly made my back ache at the end of the week.

"Forgive Me My Excuses" was me finding time for everything else before reaching this point in my life and "Have Mercy On My Repercussion" was me allowing myself to live year after year with no set goals drawing the wrong kind of attention to myself.

Because I have bragging rights of being birthed in the United States of America it proposed an opportunity to utilize the freedom of the press and even though my yearly income is below middle class standards and year in year out I had to struggle and strategize I articulate different and because books are mostly about people I'm learning to critique my subjects mainly because it's about someone and whether I'm preferring to heroes or criminals people have rights.

This by far is my favorite book because I'm writing my thoughts as I go along. Another concerning fact that I wanna address to young adults because I grew up in a rural countryish environment I wasn't face with the pressure of wanting to be famous, like young adults are today. They see the nice expensive cars, the stacks of money but they never get the chance to adjust their attitude especially if it's gonna involve the night life of clubbing. Young adults are motivated by seeing and wanting and by wanting to give their mother better they take the large lump sum offered but quickly become agitated when deductions and other expenses has to come out of their money and their safety isn't always the safest.

While I'm on safety I mentioned ridesharing earlier and due to a number of incidents and dishonest drivers lives has been taken and now safety procedures are being enforced in honor of the victims.

S-Stop plan ahead. Before you request a ride, think about where you're headed and review the safety features in the app so you know how to use them.

A-Ask, ask your driver "What's my name?" to confirm they have booked a trip with you through the ride sharing app.

M—Match, match the make, model and license plate of the car with the one displayed in the app.

I—Inform share the details of your trip with a friend. Utilize the "sharing status" function in the app.

*And always check to see if child safety locks are on.

I know exactly what I'm writing and why I'm writing and I'm not looking for validation from anyone because I have a pondering heart because this book is not written in the normal educational text as others it doesn't mean that the message isn't there. And there will come a day when we all will strive for greatness.

And life living principles can't come off as boring or without emotions because the younger generation will continue living without their most valuable assets (the mother, father, or the grandmother) and they will continue to chase after their dream.

Because I spent a large portion of my life drinking alcohol and getting high the day I was about to get sentence a judge looked beyond my problems and I remember him vaguely addressing me in utter disappointment and telling me that they will listen to you as

I told him my future plan. Because so many books are written in a highly educational format the content is over a lot of people's head to comprehend. I'm not writing to chase after a royalty check I needed more reference of job history to put on applications than just jobs worked in the past and I've spent thousands completing book projects just so one should know how involved I am. Sadly as it is to know that you can't save everybody I don't want it to be an excuse not to try. For those who was fortunate enough to skip the rough low income living before you can appreciate how you turn out "it made you tough". It made you realize no one has the time to worry about your living condition or your income. You do what everyone else do who sharing the experience "you manage". I went on for years mad at everyone else because I didn't know what it was that I wanted to do and now that I'm on the outside looking in I see everyone been comfortable. I don't want to come out of the lifestyle that caused me so much grief and not share it with those who still trying to figure it out. The same way an artist sings their heart out to get that standing ovation at the end of their song is the same form of energy and emotion I'm using to write my books.

I have been delivered and I am a living testimony and as I work from day to day and months pass by I sometimes feel like being a testimony fades out and it doesn't give me the same affect when I was first delivered and because I have a one-of-a-kind wife when she sees the discernment she reminds me that I'm a blessing and how lucky she is to have me. I guess the one thing that made my life a challenge is that I never knew what it felt like to be happy from beginning to end and because wisdom is the beginning of acquiring knowledge it provides you with the initiative to thirst in longevity criterias such as breathing, divinity, eternity, having a holy purpose, and a grace of positive energy that makes the resurrection power ask who is this? And may

I join in on making him great. If I was to say to you I bet you can't change you would most likely answer "I bet I can if I put my mind to it depending on who is making the suggestion you would answer with a strong sense of assurance that you could change example: if a friend make the suggestion to you, you would jokingly say why I need to change ain't nothing wrong with me or what I'm doing but if a judge make the suggestion and you looking at a year and he say because I believe in you Imma let you serve 5 months with 1 year of probation and 40 hrs. of community service your assurance that you can change is magnified 3x over and that's the strong will assurance I'm asking of you when it comes to the principles I'm delivering. I'm not clueless when it comes to knowing that every household isn't a loving one. Young adults who disturb others while class is being taught they either whined up suspended or in alternative school where they feel they can continue misbehaving in a more aggressive manner rather than change the attitude. It's not a fly-by-night situation to why the young adults will continue to need a peer specialist guidance to substain their performance todays parents know that their young adults are weed smokers but if the young adult never hear the parent say look, I need you to change at least until some of this chaos dies down the young adult becomes their own influence and the parent suggestions never gain its strength of authority and it continue to be withheld. Should we just allow the village of incarcerated inmates to raise and advise a parent responsibility or do we get more up close and personal. If I own a 10 carat bracelet and I decide to wear it when I put it on I'm going to make sure that it's fasten properly now if I go out and I lose the bracelet without acknowledging it 'til later that bracelet wasn't meant for me to have and that's how you gotta look at it because when someone runs across it that find is going to give off a sense of unexpected joy and they will attach it properly to their wrist with the hope of not loosing it but what are the chances that unexpected joy is the joy that's waiting deep down in most young adults the only difference "we have to be that find."

I wanna make a short insinuation about rap music I grew up listening to rap music because it was the music of my generational era. Rap music is not an added addition of a curse to humanity's evolution. It's the use of using metaphors and similes and slang to perpetuate making a long story short its far from the groovy 70's and it's not understood by most who lived before its breakthrough young girls started out writing in journals guys wrote down their ambitions "respectfully speaking it's a preference."

So much has changed my life without being physically impacted it's spiritual gratitude that makes my cup runneth over being grateful learning hereditary traits that has been freely given is nothing less than astonishing and after I'm done voicing the things that are worthy into existence my next step will be to work on voicing the retrieval. By me trying to show society my growth I wanted to do a number of things that would separate me from the abnormal interactions going on around us.

Because we don't know the exact deadline for our life we waste a lot of time contemplating on what I could of or should of done. Instead of doing. The only thing I desire to come out of this is to reset a moment of happiness in people's lives due to a lot of circumstances we lose more than we gain and everyone handle losses differently. I truly would have never thought that I would have made it thus far and I owe a substantial amount of gratitude to the prayer warriors who meditate day and night, those who anointed me, the many who gathered around me laying hands on me ridding me of unclean spirits that I may become a testimony locking away my past.

The 2 generations before me they were originals and as I grow wiser at becoming a successful author I want generations coming after me to become copy cats learn not to bottle up your anger, learn not to follow the crowd, be more hands on with your siblings that's much younger looking up to you this pen and notebook has given me the outlet that I needed being on the right medication for my disorder has helped me tremendously.

A lot of us we stick our chest out proclaiming to be a good man to our woman but when her child goes through the motions of showing signs that their unstable instead of acquiring the necessary help for them we kick 'em out. What went on between the serpent and the woman God acknowledged it by putting enmity between thee and the woman, and they seed and her seed we bypass how that course of action was him healing a difficult situation by far I am not the only one who has been robbed of happiness but I come to realize that you don't leave situations to become toxic we are at a point in time now where young adults feel if they are being treated "unfairly" then it's subject to consequences. Have you ever heard a woman who has no kids of her own and use the term "our kids" it's a deserving statement that if we plant it give it the proper nutrients "our sun" will do the rest.

Even though the people in our cities can be unpredictable we still have to deal with them as saints placing at their feet everything that can be used to navigate them. We judge books by the cover all the time and by doing so we fail to acknowledge the cries that really do need the help. Because I've been there I know a lot of people who are awaiting for light to shine through their dark, gloomy clouds that's plaguing their lives.

When we make birthday wishes or New Year's resolutions it's mainly about the individual what they want or how they gonna change and that's just it. Everyone shall desire to undergo "change" when I say have mercy on my repercussions, here's what comes to mind: "An apology means nothing if the pattern remains the same."

Book writing is the new wave for me and I want it to be invasive when it reach your mailbox your children's hand continuing family values from a new man's perspective.

You can't win the lottery if you never play and it's likely you won't succeed if you never try. I said before my books of experiences isn't the icing on the cake people who have lived horrifying street encounters has so much more to say we as writers we try to but we also leave so much out hoping that someone else has that valuable puzzle piece to complete the cause.

Do you sleep well? Knowing innocent children have lost their lives before you or someone elderly. Although Jesus answers prayers it's also our job as a new age apostle to join in assisting Him to give back the worldly results that they are seeking. Don't walk through a forest if you don't have the necessary tools to find your way because when anxiety causes you to panic and starvation cause you to thirst by chance someone will run across you giving you the assisting attention you need. Life is confusing when you can go anywhere in the States and everything appears to be the same. I have a wife and children of my own. I don't look to be fathered but all of my fatherly qualities they have to come from someone who knows humanity before I was birthed in it or ever planned to become one.

One of the scariest things about this life we are always willing to risk our livelihood to get involved with someone we have no clue of who they really are and it only whines up making what was supposed to be the simplest form of affection that much harder to embrace the next because of our flaws and our mischievous ways of how we respond when they are highlighted it steals the spotlight from those who just want a deserving chance and when too many things are highlighted at one time it's hard to get the focus back on what's more rewarding.

Everything that's made has a reaction to another an earthquake won't shake great distances if the earth magnetic plates doesn't slide above and beneath one another. A volcano doesn't erupt on a daily basis. Pressure and heat has to build up and release gases that centuries had founded prior to keeping it cool up to the point of explosion. Death is not the human's reaction we make it that because a lot of us don't practice the ways of old. We chase after what's new that doesn't even have a steady foundation. Do you know how many foundations there are for children that has been murdered just by gun violence alone? Along more than you can count on both hands. What's right? Some choosing to come together, brainstorming how to alleviate more pain and suffering from taking place or a form of retaliation that causes civilians to dislike authority figures, entice lootings and public vandalism none of which will bring the dead back but the possibility of gathering the few age groups and making sure that the time has been spent correctly enforcing understanding people who are likely to attend meaningful functions usually not the ones who go out and commit crimes involving other civilians. It's those who think that their a priority within their social friends, it's those who has their ear to the street whenever a verdict is finalized, it's those who are willing to leave their family behind to participate in mayhem instead of a healthy practice. Are we allowing what's right to become irrelevant? Keep in mind nothing exist as it appears. Because we have lost so many forerunners who fought devoutly for civil rights. The tax on a bottle of liquor, a pack of cigars, or a case of beer gives us a definitely outlook on what's in vain and what's not.

If I live long enough to sit back and listen to a percentage of my readers tell how I helped impacted their lives that would be a victory that I never thought, I could accomplish when I was down and on my last leg tired and exhausted.

People didn't refuse me they even went above and beyond so that I can live more of a stable life. Me writing just seems like the best way to say to so many that I'm appreciative. I can't allow myself to go back to how it was for me to be delivered is a one-time ordeal for me I won't allow temptation to persuade me that he did it one time before he'll do it again naïve people most times don't make it long enough to do it again. I survived a storm that I couldn't see my hand in front of my face but I could hear others yelling at the highest tone of their voice is anyone else out here because we need rescuing.

The reason why I'm pushing the issue of understanding in my writings because some who abuses alcohol only thinks that their harming themselves not realizing that the spirit that dwells on the inside of us can report back without warning if its life is feeling control due to carelessness we don't have enough time here on earth to correct everyone of our flaws but we can engage to a higher calling who will gather our imperfections and allow us to reset our lives for a purposeful living I'm asking you to join me in teaching younger generations.

That giving up is not an option that suicide is not the answer, that street drugs will consume you and violence of any type will silence them. If there is a man who feel that he's being withheld from seeing his kids maybe because the woman do 90% of our responsibility. Cook for them, shop for them, pick 'em up, drop 'em off, keep scheduled doctors' appointments, throw 'em birthday parties, attend graduations, get 'em prom ready. Ask yourself I'm I doing enough? And if you answer no you know why her time is occupied from sun up to sundown and if you just gonna sit there with a beer in your hand and a blunt to your lips then what's the use you can freely do that with the homeboys but if you are sincere about wanting to be involved I hope however this book reaches you it has enough insights that you won't waste anymore time due to self-infliction allowing the truths in this book to solidify your place in their life.

Here's a couple of things that we do know we know it's extremely hard to find the right words to say to someone who has lossed a child or a beloved love one we know we can successfully coach someone from a suicide attempt and we know how to embrace a foster child giving them the assurance that no one will ever hurt them again and each of these has to come from insights and conversation that's considered ethical.

Don't become exceedingly over joyed because you made it to success, become exceedingly over joyed because your readers/listeners doesn't have to make an assumption of who they think you are your now accessible to show them.

Although a book may not be your first alternative when going up against a pair of new sneakers or a video game but for whatever reason my book(s) reach you I hope that it gives you clarity and even though my insights and advice may not be as accurate of those of your respected family member you're going to one day become the head of household and your members will seek from you.

It's regularly people will try to find something wrong with the ones who has your best interest mainly it's because they want you to remain vulnerable and assessable to them.

This book gonna gain the attention of (2) types of people those that will invite you which is about a number game and braggin' rights and the other is those that will include you.

Although, I may not affect as many as I originally anticipated I will continue to man handle the explanation of ineffectiveness because it's an ethical responsibility that makes a human purpose a value of importance.

* You may not agree with every thing
I say just respect what I stand for *

Printed in the United States
by Baker & Taylor Publisher Services

Printed in the United States
by Baker & Taylor Publisher Services